EVERYDAY AUTHOR CHALLENGE

BIBLE DEVOTIONAL

JEN LOWRY

Table of Contents

Everyday Author Challenge Bible Devotional

Jen Lowry

Monarch Educational Services, L.L.C.
Clayton, NC

Everyday Author Challenge Bible Devotional
By Jen Lowry

Cover Designer: Monarch Educational Services, L.L.C.

Everyday Author Challenge Bible Devotional/First Edition 2019

Summary: Finding time to write in our busy life can sometimes be a challenge. We can feel unmotivated, tired, and uninspired, even when it's time to sit down to write because we are so on the go. This Bible devotional is a challenge to all authors struggling to find the work-life-write balance from a best-selling author who is figuring it all out. Jen will challenge you to honor your blank page. Get ready. It's time to share your story.

{1. Christian Nonfiction 2. Bible Devotional 3. Author 4. Journal 5. Christianity 6. Faith 7. Hope 8. Reflections 9. Challenge 10. Testimony 11. Encouragement 12. Writing 13. Publishing

Typography by Monarch Educational Services, L.L.C.

7654321

Monarch Educational Services, L.L.C.
Clayton NC

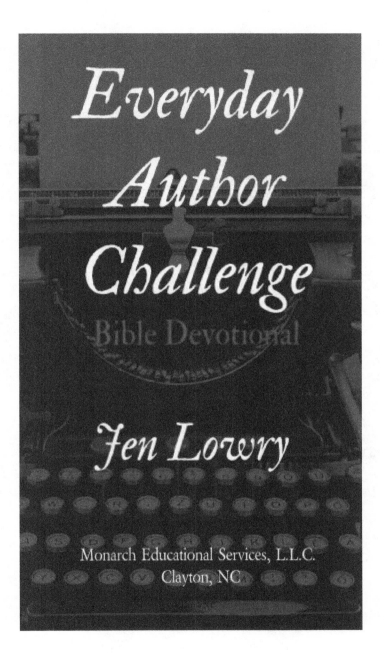

Everyday Author Challenge

Bible Devotional

Jen Lowry

Monarch Educational Services, L.L.C.
Clayton, NC

I can do all
things through
Christ who
strengthens
me.
Phillipians 4:13

A Challenge a Day Keeps Writer's Block Away

Guiding Bible Verse: *"Let us not become weary in doing good, for at the proper time we will reap a harvest if we do not give up." Galatians 6:9*

WHAT CAN I SAY? I'M a challenge driven woman. This isn't my first challenge devotional, and I feel the Lord will continue to motivate me in these small ways to keep me intentionally and purposefully serving Him with a smile. My life is a daily challenge, so I don't use this term flippantly or light in any way. I take on each task before me with praise and prayer on my lips. I don't always get it right but I sure do try. I'm a coffee drinking momma, wife, Christian, best-selling author of clean books for all ages, full time literacy coach, English I teacher, homeschool administrator, cook, maid, chauffeur, business owner, and author coach.

You're probably saying, "Yeah right. How can you be all those things?"

Because I am all of those things and more. The challenges I create for myself keep me motivated. They keep me focused on the task set before me or I would choose a different route with my time – like binge watching episode shows in my pajamas. We all have a default button. That's mine

I'm an author and must write. I have to find the time, but how? I wake up at 5:30 am and don't stop until almost eleven at night. If only I could stop the hands of time and still be able to move through the motions. If only there were two of me. Think about all I could accomplish. Bottom line. There is one me. I can't stop time. I have no control over many things that are going on in my life right now.

That isn't sad. That's just the way life is. I need to work to have an income to provide for my family. I have family responsibilities that are a top priority for me.

But I also have to write. It's not an "I want to write" kinda feeling that hits me early in the morning. It's the "I need to write," and it's a way I ground myself to this world without floating away.

I imagine my life without writing, and it just doesn't make sense to me. It's hard to fathom it. It's not something I ever want to face. I see a blank page and all the mysteries it holds for me, and I am must go after it with a passion put to good use.

I am so many things other than the list I created above. That's just the tip of the iceberg. I know it's the same for you. There are so many ways we could *I am* ourselves it could probably fill up the pages of an entire book. In fact, that's your first challenge. Write an *I Am* poem. In all the ways that you are, you are an author. You are a writer. Make sure you give yourself an identifying literary connection that gives honor to your passion for writing.

I want you to not go any further in this devotional until you complete the first challenge.

CHALLENGE:

Don't turn the page. Grab your journal. Page one. Write your *I Am* poem. Begin.

After you complete your *I Am* poem, write the following verse in your journal and write a reflection.

"See what great love the Father has lavished on us, that we should be called children of God! And that is what we are!" 1 John 3:1

We are children of God. I am a child of God. Recognizing who we are and whose we are can break our fears, uncertainties, and doubts. Let us praise God for the gift He's given us, his Son, and our salvation. Before we move further, if you don't know Jesus as your Savior, you can say this prayer with me and begin a new journey of faith this very day. You belong to God, call out to Him, and He will hear your cry. He will rescue you.

DEAR GOD,

Thank you for your Word. Thank you for the hope it brings. I believe in you. I believe in Jesus Christ. I believe He died for my sins and rose from the dead. I believe He cares for me and forgives me. I believe He loves me. Help me to live this life for you. Teach me the ways that I should go. In Jesus name I pray, Amen.

If you said that prayer to Jesus for the first time, you have been saved. Your eternity will be in Heaven. Your hope will be found in the love and grace of the Lord. Share your testimony with others. Email me because I'd love to hear it! Share the good news. Jesus is alive and one day will return. Be ready.

How does the call to salvation connect with an author journey? Once you come to the fullness of the knowledge this writing life is a calling, a special assignment, an anointing that not all have, you'll hear the words of Jesus with new meaning, *"The harvest is plentiful but the workers are few." (Matthew 9:37)*

Let us work our author life for the Lord. In all we do, let us praise Him, show our gratitude, and spread kindness. I am more than just an author. At first, when I started my own journey, I hid behind so many other identifies and might drop the word author in there or maybe I wouldn't. It was almost as if I were ashamed to say it aloud for fear of what people might say. It took me a year. I'm asking you to pray about it today. This is a liberating step I wish someone would have encouraged me to take long ago.

Having belief in yourself, your capabilities, and your story helps to fuel your passion to go after your author dreams. If you don't believe in your story, who else will? If you can't champion your characters, no one else will care? You must move past the word "writing as a hobby" and reframe your mind to speak "author career."

See what great love the Father has lavished on us, that we should be called children of God! And that is what we are! 1 John 3:1

CHALLENGE CONTINUED:

After you've written your *I Am* poem, circle the word author in the poem. If you didn't write down that you were an author in your *I Am* poem, add a new line. Highlight it. Underline it. Bold it to 70 size font. Change it to your favorite color. Let the word seep into your Spirit. Repeat it.

"Author."

"I am an author."

You are not an aspiring author. You are not a hopeful writer. You are not a soon-to-be novelist working on your WIP (Work in Progress).

YOU ARE AN AUTHOR.

Period.

End of discussion about that.

If you go on line and ask around the writing community, "What makes an author legitimately an author?"

Some will answer that you must have a paid sale for your work, others will argue it's when you get a publishing contract, and then you'll have those believers like me that say it happens when your first word hits the page. If you disagree with me on this statement, then we shall continue to move forward together in this devotional. That's fine. We can agree to disagree. I was an author back in 8th grade. I just didn't believe in myself. I didn't go after my author dreams. They stayed buried within me, even though I didn't claim to be an author. In my heart, I always knew. Books were meant for me. I was meant for them.

You might not think this is a big deal, but trust me, it is. To identify ourselves as a child of God is a big deal. To call out that we are an author to strangers and family members and colleagues is a big deal. We need to begin to recognize the gift that being an author truly is. We didn't just wake up one morning saying, "I want to be an author because teaching isn't cutting it."

I bet each one of us knows where our author story first began. It might have been a long time ago after reading a book that totally took our breath away. It could have been this creeping crawling thing that started to wiggle our fingertips. It might have been the time when you had that one teacher in elementary or middle school that challenged you to write a poem or you wrote your first story because they believed in you. You might've started this journey this very day. But it wasn't because your day job wasn't making the grade and you knew you could be an overnight success and make the big bucks.

It's because of your calling.

This author life for us isn't by chance. We can't help ourselves. We are motivated by a power not of our own doing or even our own control. Don't call that fate or because your aunt was once a famous author and it must run in your bloodline. Call it a gift. Call it a treasured anointing from the Lord to do His work in the special way that is YOU.

When you connect the word author with God and author with gifting, then it's more than just a hobby. It's a way of being. The sounds of the keyboard are like heartbeats. You're breathing life into a blank page. You take nothing and turn it into something beautiful. Something that matters. Jesus was a carpenter, and I can imagine him holding a piece of wood in his hand and carving it into something special. I see us as His handiwork. He's shaped us into these quirky beings who love the sound of words like quirky running through our head. We are like a carpenter. We are dream speakers, word weavers, and tale spinners that connect emotion, feeling, thought, and heartbeats together into one thread and craft it into something special.

But how much do you identify with that part of yourself? Do you consider it hidden? Do you not want to boast or feel as if you don't have anything to show for it, so better not speak it? Do you have fears of what others would say, so you don't tell your story? If you don't tell your story, you dishonor the gift God gave you. You waste it. It's precious. Claim it. Hold on to it. Cultivate it. It will grow. Just have faith.

Let the words author come easily out of your mouth. Jesus doesn't want you to hide your gifts. He gave them to you for a purpose. When you don't identify with the gift, you really are saying you are not good enough for God's work. And we know that's not the case.

We are God's vessel and His hands and feet. His hands. His fingers. His words. Let us give our author life to God. Let us turn to God today and say this simple prayer:

"God, I give you my author life. I thank you for blessing me with writing. I love it, Lord. I am pursuing my dreams, and you know the desire of my heart. You have gifted me with something special. Help me use these gifts to glorify you. Amen."

———— ❧ ————

JOURNAL REFLECTION:

Write about your own author journey. Think of your author creation story. When did the writing bug first begin with you? What had you hooked? What inspired you? What pivotal moment in your life led you to this very day where you are an author, challenging yourself for more?

After writing your reflection, share it with the writing community. Write a blog. Post it on social media in a thread. Start a conversation. Connect with other authors by asking about their own author journey. Not only will sharing your story be an inspiration to others, it's just downright interesting to hear about how one first begins a thing. That *thing* meaning your author heart.

Share it with me. Email me your journal reflection at jenlowrywrites@gmail.com because I would love to read your story. I'd love to choose some to be on my website, to honor you and your story. Happy journaling.

Ways to Track Your Challenge

1. The next time someone asks you to tell them a little bit about yourself, identify yourself as an author.

1. Change all of your social media accounts to say author. Share out your author story after you journal. Follow me @jenlowrywrites, and I'll follow you back!

1. Each day, repeat this verse, "Looking unto Jesus, the author and finisher of our faith, who for the joy that was set before Him endured the cross, despising the shame, and has sat down at the right hand of the throne of God." Hebrews 12:2 You'll remember who is truly the author of our lives and be more mindful of how He called you to do the same.

1. Create a daily list of writing goals. Focus on what you can accomplish each day and give yourself some grace when you need to rearrange or move some items around or to another day. Celebrate small victories. Thank Jesus for giving you a blank page, and praise Him when he gives you the first word. Continue to praise as you write.

1. Journal each day. Find time to write about your author journey, your learning, motivations, inspirations, books...I could keep going here. Journaling is important and I'm going to ask you to keep up with this on a daily basis. You can thank me now or later. Either way is fine. We'll do this challenge together and stick to it.

1. Find an accountability partner. Let them know you're on a writing mission. You have a blank page before you. You have obstacles. Prayer can move that mountain in front of you and having a prayer warrior friend alongside you will help keep you on track.

1. Never give up. This is the first chapter, and I'm telling you to never stop writing. Yes, there is a lot that goes into this life. It's not an easy road. It's filled with potholes and wrong turns, construction, and roadblocks.

But once you break away from all of that and are holding the finished product in your hand – your book – your baby – your creation with the help of the Holy Spirit, you'll realize that journey you struggled with was well worth it. In fact, you might be ready that very day to start on a sequel or a new idea develops and you run with it before the ink dries on the book in your hand. Once you start, never give up. When you never give up, you produce results. Guess what that result will be? Your words will be in print. Your name will be on the cover of a book. More than that, your story will be shared with others and can help lift them up from a dark place. You can help them to escape into your world for a while and give them the hope that you found in books. But if you give up, that person loses that chance. That very person that needed your book, your story, your character, your heart on a page. Do it for Jesus. Do it for that one person. The rest will work itself out in the end.

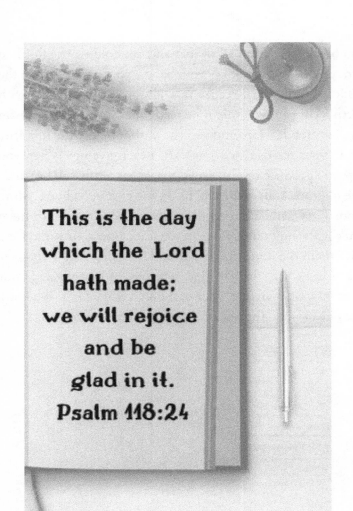

This is the day
which the Lord
hath made;
we will rejoice
and be
glad in it.
Psalm 118:24

Never Too Late to Start Now

Guiding Bible Verse: *"And he said, "Jesus, remember me when you come into your kingdom." Luke 23:42*

YOU MIGHT BE WONDERING why I started you off with such a guiding Bible verse. The convicted man on the cross beside Jesus knew there was no chance left for him. He was dying. His fate was sealed and the agony was rising. His final destination was still uncertain. Imagine what he could have been thinking through painful gasps and shock, "This is no man, this is the Messiah. Remember me in paradise." He built his courage to speak those last words to our Savior. And it wasn't too late to enter into the kingdom of Heaven.

When I knew I wanted to write this devotional to authors out there in the world, I wanted to break through any doubts or fears. What excuses did I once use for myself? What held me back from following God's call on my life?

You don't know my circumstance. It's too late.

It's not too late for you to start writing now. When I say now, I'm serious. Right now. Here's your challenge:

Grab your journal, a blank piece of paper, or a blank page Word document. Look at how beautiful it is. It's beckoning you.

"Trust in the LORD with all thine heart; and lean not unto thine own understanding. In all thy ways acknowledge him, and he shall direct thy paths." Proverbs 3:5-6

Before the blank page, sit a few minutes with Jesus. Pray to Him to guide you in your paths. Tell Him the desires of your heart. He will hear you. He knows your story. It's already inside of you. It's not out there somewhere floating on Pluto. It's buried within you, the very heart of you knows it already. It's already planned and plotted and the course is sure. You just have a blank page. That's actually a good thing. It means you can allow the work to be done as it's meant to be.

But I don't have the right situation to be writing at this very moment. I think I'll put it off some more.

It's never too late, and the Bible tells us we aren't promised tomorrow because you don't know what your next day will bring (Proverbs 27:1).

But...

But nothing. No more excuses. I already set you up from the first chapter getting you to identify with the word author. In this chapter, I've set you in front of a blank page. You have to figure this life out so that you can get your writing time.

But how? My time is limited! I have so much on my plate already. How can I do this writing life, too?

When you follow your passions and what God has gifted for you to accomplish, it will not feel like work. It will be a blessing to you, a relief in times of trouble, a pick-me-up, and filled with gratitude.

It's all how you look at this writing life that makes the difference. If you stare in front of you and see all of the obstacles, then you are more likely to quit. Stop that. Stop doing that today. Yes, there are issues you will face. There will be frustrating moments or doubts that creep in. Let's get real smack in the middle of Chapter 2. We are human. We can fall into this automatic pilot of despair. We can spiral and start excuses that can never end.

But, with the guidance of the Holy Spirit and the focus and determination, we can also see a clear view in front of us.

"He said to them, "Because of your little faith. For truly, I say to you, if you have faith like a grain of mustard seed, you will say to this mountain, 'Move from here to there,' and it will move, and nothing will be impossible for you." Matthew 17:20

If you see a mountain of excuses piling in front of you, pray for Jesus to help you move them out of your way. If you see yourself standing in your own way, pray for the Lord to be able to help you reframe your mind for the work set before you.

You are an author, and I'm hoping you've been saying that to yourself since I tried to implant it into your brain from the beginning of this devotional. I have no magic or special science fiction tools to control your brain, only prayer, and

I'm praying for you. I pray for every reader of this book to recognize that we must all stop making excuses about why we aren't going after our blank page and turning it into something new. Something. Anything. A first line. A brainstorm list. An image that inspires you. A dedication page. Something. Anything. Begin.

Dear Lord,

Let me stop making excuses about why I'm not writing. Let me write to serve you, Lord. Help me with my time. Help me with priorities. Help me see how I can make this work so that I can fit it in. Lord, I don't see a way but I know you have a way for me. I'm trusting in you to reveal your plan to me. Amen.

JOURNAL REFLECTION:

What writing excuses are standing in your way? For every excuse write a new belief statement under each one. Challenge yourself to start small and tackle one excuse at a time.

Give back to her as she has given; pay her back double for what she has done. Pour her a double portion from her own cup.
Revelations 18:6

Tools for the Trade

Guiding Bible Verse: *"And my God will meet all your needs according to the riches of his glory in Christ Jesus." Philippians 4:19*

So, now you want to write. Now what? You don't go out to plant a garden without having tools. Even a spoon is better than nothing to plant a seed.

I was asked the question over the summer by a sweet sister in Christ who was ready to start her first page. "What do you use to write a book?"

This is not a question to roll your eyes at. We don't know what we don't know. And many people look to the author world and think of it as a great mystery. I was once one of those people.

Talking about excuses: I was the biggest excuse maker in the world. I would hold print copies of books in my hand and question: How does it get from head to cream pages? Talk about one of the greatest mysteries in the world.

Not really. I'm here to step into the gap and help you out.

Unless you research this writing life, it's not common knowledge. It's not like I could go to colleagues or family or friends and rattle off questions and find a mentor within my circle. No one in my immediate line knew the first thing about writing. I had no writing groups. I was from a town of a thousand friends, our motto, but no writing friends. So, I spent years holding books in my hands and dreaming of my own name on a cover.

But how do I start the ball rolling? What are the steps?

1. You're an author now. You are speaking that to yourself since Chapter 1. I'm going to keep repeating this.
2. You have a blank page before you or better yet, you have some words on a page before you since Chapter 2.
3. You will begin building your researching skills today.

One of the great ones I would always fall back on was, "I don't know where to start?" Even with research, who can you trust? What's credible? Are there reliable sources out there or is it gimmicky, where people are just trying to make money of someone, exploiting naive authors into thinking the next best thing is just a click away?

For those out there not immersed in the writing community, even the question of where to start might be daunting. What tools of the trade are the best and what resources are now available for authors to do the task set before them?

I started with *Word* on my laptop. I already had the program. It has the typical spell/grammar check included. It shows levels at the end of my document for grade level estimations and readability for my target audience. I often update my saved documents and place them in *Google Folders*. Long ago, I had a computer crash and my manuscripts disappeared in a flash. That lesson taught me to save often, email to myself, and now save to *Google Drive*.

I know authors who also use *Google Docs* if they don't have *Word* because it's free online with a *Google* account. You can type on the go without having to worry about backing up your files. I share *Google Docs* with my beta readers (Definition of beta readers: willing and trusted readers who provide me with valuable input, edits, and proof my work in real time as I type).

Other writers use a program they purchase call Scrivener, a word processing tool for authors I've never looked into this writing program because I'm satisfied with what works for me but many authors scream it from the rooftops. It's one you can add to your list to check out. Research it, and see if it's right for you.

Wait, you won't tell me which one? I thought you'd just say – do this and do that, and I'd do it.

You've got to do **YOUR** thing, and I want you to know you don't have to go out there and spend tons of upfront money on anything fancy in order to share your story with the world.

My thing might not be your thing. I will tell you to research and the ways I do it so that at least you can jumpstart your work. But I want to be honest with you upfront. A lot about life is trial and error. You get that. We figure things out as we go. As we invest time in the writing community, we learn more about it, and we grow. We add tools to our toolbox. We try new things and some work, some don't. We keep trying. We never give up and guess what, eventually, it will be to the point where we can clearly say – "This works for me." It might not be today, but it's coming. I know it.

Researching tools of the trade is something you need to invest time in. Starting a web search, trying out free trials, and watching YouTube videos where authors share their insider tricks and tips – can be a great place to start.

I have a daily podcast, <u>Jen Lowry Writes</u> on nine different podcast platforms where I share my author journey and have connected with a wonderful community of authors through this podcast adventure. An author emailed me to let me know all about the wonders of ProWritingAid. I was using Grammarly as a spell checker for awhile but when I met *ProWritingAid*, I knew I needed both tools to help with my editing process.

The great news about these extensions or add-ons to your existing *Word* or *Google Doc* is there's a free version, and you can try it out, research it, and learn it before you upgrade. Who doesn't like free? I'm all about it. I'm a North Carolina teacher by day on a budget with no pay raise in sight, remember. I'm on a lockdown mode when it comes to my finances. My tools I find and share are always free. Of course, you can easily upgrade when you're ready but it's great to start with the free versions first to see what you think and investigate it for yourself. Personally, I loved ProWritingAid so much I did go with the subscription, but it's not a necessity. My author friends use the straight up free version for initial edits.

So, when you go out there researching the tools for writing, remember I started small and easy. I started free. It works for me. *Word + ProWritingAid* (free) + *Grammarly* (free) = the book you are holding in your hand. It's that easy.

Or is it?

The greatest tool I have is not a trick or computer program, and it's definitely not something that can be bought in a store. It is freely given, and again, I'm emphasizing the word FREE here.

"But the Advocate, the Holy Spirit, whom the Father will send in my name, will teach you all things and will remind you of everything I have said to you." John 14:26

That means I depend upon the Holy Spirit to not only supply the tools I need to live this author life, challenge and support others, but to also teach me the things I need to keep moving in a forward direction.

With each new day, I've got a new uphill climb. It's a new page. A blank one. That's not only fascinating to me, but also a little scary. I'll admit writing your story might not be the easiest thing you've tried to accomplish, but I can tell you with all certainty it'll be worth it.

So, now that you know what tools I use, the most important being the Holy Spirit, what next? You've got to just type it. You've got to get it on the page. No matter what it sounds like. You can't edit something that hasn't made its way to the paper yet. You can't move forward until you position your hands over keys. Is it that simple? Yes.

Type it even though you face uphill challenges. Type it because you've been called to do it. It's not a hobby. It's a pursuit of your passion and purpose.

Type it.

Ray Bradbury (one of my favorite authors of all time) rented a typewriter in a basement. Libraries have computers for use. It may be timed, but if you write a little each day after a while, you'll have a whole lot. Give it a shot.

Let's say you have the fancy tools at your disposal. You have a laptop or a desktop in an office. You've got programs set up to support your work like *Scrivener* (never used it but many authors do) or *ProWritingAid* (love it) or *Grammarly* (adore it) or SAS Writing Reviser (just learned about it). Many free version addons work well on your Word or Google products. Use that old grammar checker on Word. Figure it out as you go! But go.

Type it.

There is a blank page in front of you. Even if it's a napkin or an old receipt you stuck in your purse, along with ten others. Maybe you want to start blogging first, and get your first taste of writing before jumping straight into a novel or nonfiction work for your business.

Maybe you want to collect poetry and share your heart and passion for the written and spoken word. You might not be ready to talk about publishing yet. That's GREAT! In fact, all authors started at the same place you're sitting in right now, staring at a blank page.

Isn't that comforting to know this. It's not a big mystery. It's following a call. It's stepping up in faith and letting go all the way. Let go of fear, of excuses, doubt, or worry. This takes time. It might not be today when you let all of that go because that takes self-discipline and dependency, but you can start writing today.

So, you're ready to write. Let's talk about this.

Now what?

You decide what works for you. You can spend all day long reading someone's writing advice on how to get started on your perfect novel that is guaranteed to sale and all these online courses or webinars, but the bottom line is, you've got to do YOU.

Just be you. Figure you out.

It's wonderful to hear advice, learn from models, and study the author world. I do it all the time. I'm not discouraging that at all. In fact, I'm asking you to make it a part of a new routine you set for yourself to study and grow in this author life. What I am warning you against is to not lose YOU in the process.

Be your authentic self.

But how?

Many authors place themselves into two categories. I'm sure it's not always so neatly packaged and there can be exceptions to the rule but the talk of the writing community revolves around the question:

Are you an architect or a gardener?

I like those two words way better than pantser or plotter, but they mean the same thing? I like the word gardener because it conjures up childhood memories. In fact, I have so many fond memories of walking rows of my grandmother's garden that I wrote a children's picture book in her memory called *Myrtle's Garden* just for her and the students I teach.

Journal Reflection:

Go to YouTube and listen to a beautiful hymn, "I Come to the Garden Alone," by one of your favorite artists. I particularly love the versions by Mahalia Jackson or Alan Jackson. Both Jackson's and both allow my spirit to fall into this calm serenity to focus. How does this song remind you of writing?

I show up to the garden. I'm not walking it alone. Jesus is with me. I pray as I enter into the gates of my garden. The landscape might appear to be rough to the outsider, but it all makes sense to me. I stare at space. I let the fingers roam free. I set them loose on the soil. They squirm and dance like earthworms fighting against the light. They scurry and dive under the earth and do their magic. Themes emerge and I think of those as planting seeds.

Themes are lessons our readers will take away with them after we are long from their hands or ears if they listen to your audiobook. Those seeds matter.

Even if you're an architect by nature and organize your entire book, I still want to encourage you to think of yourself as a gardener as well. What we plant within the pages of our book can do something even more than we could imagine. Gardening isn't predictable. It depends upon variables. Sometimes it's out of our control, and we don't fight it.

That's when it morphs into something more than we ever imagined we could write on our own because in fact we aren't alone while we write. What a joy it is to know the Holy Spirit is with us right now while we read and write, challenge each other and journal.

It's me and you together on this journey.

"For where two or three gather in my name, there am I with them." Matthew 18:20

But what about a topic? How do I know what to write about? This is all up to you, and when you are being your authentic self, you can't hide from what you love.

It naturally exists within us.

Journal Reflection:

What are you most passionate about? Do you have a particular expertise in an area that you'd love to share with the world? Do you own a business and wish you had something for your clientele? How do you mist help others and how could that fit within the pages of a book? What book have you read and wished you'd written it? What movie did you watch and wish you could've changed it? What do you love to read? What sparks your thoughts and lets your imagination run wild? What is it that you love to watch on television? What story has always been skating around in your head but you never thought about writing it down? What conversations do you find yourself most engaged in? Where do you think you shine the most? What do you think is lacking on the current bookshelf in your home right now?

Make a list of all of these questions in your journal and go after each one with prayer on your lips, with a YouTube gospel soundtrack playing in the background, and let go! What landed on the page?

We let the story be. We honor the blank page. It comes to life right in front of an author as a tangible thing. Like virtual reality, a story performed on a stage, an apparition floating around us. It makes sense. It comes together and it will for you, too. Don't feel like you need a working title for your novel or book to get started. That can come way later in the process. You need one word, one first sentence, one page...that leads into the next and into the next.

But how?

With prayer.

Prayer and dependency upon God. He'll take you to the answers you seek. Not this book. Not any course or class or self-help guide. The Lord will take you exactly where you need to be, and help you to honor the blank page. I want to challenge your thinking. I want you to imagine a seed. You are the seed. Everything within you is ready. The story is there. It just needs nurturing. It needs a place to feel secure, covered, and protected.

You need to find the place where you can be vulnerable. Writing is your heart on your sleeve all the time. It's a place where your heart beats, and because of that, if you let it, you can also let your heart bleed.

Protecting your heart can only be found in the knowing that you're writing for a higher purpose, a heavenly reward. We write because it's the Holy Spirit prompting us to do so. It's not on a whim, and it's not a hobby.

It's a calling that needs to be answered. Finding yourself in your garden can be the first step towards discovering your voice, your story, and your style.

That's the life of an author who gardens their way through it, is an author that knows dependency upon outside forces is a requirement for their harvest or a successful crop. I've never heard of a successful farmer without irrigation or rain. I don't want to be without the living water. I never want my well to run dry.

"If you knew the gift of God and who it is that asks you for a drink, you would have asked him and he would have given you living water." John 4:10

Now, if you want to know what it's like to be an "author architect," we need to go out there and ask others. I can't think like that. I can't plan or organize or draw blue prints or sketches of plot diagrams or beats. There are great plotters out there than can give you all the tools of the trade, the books to read like *Save the Cat*, or you can study to learn the structural patterns of story. It's not that I can't. I just don't work that way. It's not me. Remember when I told you that you must find out who you are.

There isn't a personality test on this one that I can give to you because just because you might run a tight ship and organize the heck out of your life, that doesn't mean you'll necessarily pull out those same attributes when you set before a page to write.

The whole story comes within you someway, somehow. Whether you need to draw it out, design it, make outline notes, or just wing it. It's coming. Get ready, because I'm praying for you to take hold of the greatest tool you'll ever need – the Holy Spirit.

That's next. That's the challenge. Imagine I'm Yoda, and I'm sending you on a quest to find your true author self. You must use the force for this one. The force of will, determination, and with the guidance of the Holy Spirit, you'll figure you out. Only then can you begin the journey called writing. It's comparable to a faith journey. You'll be free to express yourself in the way in which you are meant to be. It's pretty much the old-fashioned finding out what works for you.

But that means you have to start.

Start writing. See where it takes you. You'll know if it's right. You'll figure out pretty quick if it's not, or maybe you won't, but you'll be writing.

I want to tell you a quick story (those of you that listen to the Jen Lowry Writes podcast know it might not be so quick...I talk a lot...). Last summer, I felt I had a fantastic, thrilling idea for a novel. I researched the mess out of the topic while I was writing. YouTube videos played in the background on cult stories, serial killers, and exiting cult life.

I read real life stories and news articles. I would write a chapter and take a break to research. I'd go back into it, capturing my character's teenage voice and knowing this was shaping up to be something unique.

Until Chapter 11. I made it right smack in the middle and became convicted – I wasn't supposed to be writing this. It wasn't right for me. It didn't fit me. It was very dark and twisting in ways I didn't feel comfortable taking a reader. I didn't feel safe writing about it.

It's not that it wasn't clean, but there was no light. There was no place where redeeming qualities could shine. It was spiraling further down into murder and a dark abyss, and I stared at the scene I just wrote and started to do the one thing I wouldn't have imagined doing at the beginning of the work.

I deleted the file.

I thought it was going to turn out to be my next YA horror. Instead, it went into my recycling bin to be deleted forever.

It was a work that would never see the light of day. Then, new work fell in its place. Do I regret the time spent on it? Nope, not at all. It taught me valuable lessons. It taught me to trust the Holy Spirit whispers. When the Spirit said, "Nope." I obeyed.

Deleting the work did feel a little strange but it was also rewarding. I felt surer in the direction I knew I needed to go down. I wasn't a suspense thriller writer. It wasn't in me to produce that type of work. I might love to watch documentaries and horror movies, but maybe if I just sat in front of a blank page again, something else would come along and become my next adventure.

And it did. Thirteen books in total. The cult book is not included, and that's fine. You can abandon work, just like you can come back to old work and revise it, or create something new.

Let's begin. Right now. Go to the computer and pull up a new Word document or Google Doc.

CHALLENGE:

If you are still unsure after prayer, reflections, and time, start talking out ideas. Share them with a relative, close friend, or write them in your journal. Read in the genre you love. Spend time in author craft work and view author videos on YouTube. Find places where you can go where you feel particularly inspired, a garden or nature hike, a place that brings you joy, and take along your journal with you to take notes.

Cast all your
anxiety on
him because
he cares
for you.
1 Peter 5;7

Building Your Author Platform

"*C ast all your anxiety on him because he cares for you.*" *1 Peter 5:7*

WHEN AUTHORS DISCUSS their next steps with me, they often think it's going straight from novel to editor to query to agent, as if it is this linear walk that perfectly aligns with stars. When I tell them that they have to simultaneously build their author platform while they are considering a story structure or writing the first draft of their WIP, they have the misconception that it's too early to do all that.

I've got time, they think. I disagree with this sentiment. Carry the writing community and readers with you from brainstorm to writing to completion. Build your author platform, and start it today.

It's never too early to build a potential relationship with fellow readers, authors, and those involved in the writing community.

This is where you've got to figure out the next step of the author world. You're writing now. You've got a new document in front of you or an old story you pulled out of your trunk. You've got words on a page. You are working a writing routine and getting that thing figured out, or maybe not, but you're trying to figure it out. Congratulations.

You ask, *Isn't that enough?*

No.

It's not. You need to really take this challenge seriously and listen very closely. Don't wait until your novel is finished to do this. START TODAY.

What do you want me to start?

I'm glad you asked. You will build your author platform. Platform = readers. It's that simple. Wrap your head around this. If you don't build a platform, no one will know about you. Sure, you are telling people at your job now that you're an author. Your family knows your investing time and energy in following your passion. But what about the millions of readers? How will they know you? I'd love to puff you up and tell you that you're a big fish in a tiny pond, but you know that I'm just speaking tall tales there. We are small fish in a gigantic publishing industry.

Does that mean it's hopeless? NO WAY.

In fact, you will find a reader out there just waiting for the next best book written especially for them. And I have a pretty good feeling you're ready to write it. How do you connect with them? It will be through the work you put in with your platform building.

You are skill stacking. You are building a tower with many offices. You push the elevator to take you to each floor. You get off and say hi and check in, and you get back on the elevator and head to the top office with the magnificent view. You sit above the floors knowing that all the work is being done. You set it in motion. You let it live and be and bank. Once you post or record or share, it doesn't go away. It becomes a part of your office space, your story. One follower will turn to two will turn into thousands. Give it time.

Let me remind you again. This is not hopeless and it's not hard. If it were hard, I wouldn't have you doing it. It's actually FUN. It's not time consuming, only if you let it get away from you. Remember, you're in control of how you spend your time. You have to learn to manage your time. Writing is a priority. You can't promote something you don't write. However, you can't promote something on a platform you don't have. I hope I'm making myself clear. This isn't an option. It's a given. It's an expectation.

Think of this work leading to the perfect conclusion. There will be a person waiting for you at the book signing or event you'll hold one day, with your book in your hand. How did they find out about you? Who spreads the news? How did they hear about your event? Who shared out your status? What new follower became your fan? What new connection helped open a door for you? It all has to start somewhere.

Might as well be today.

You need to build up your base. Your home teams. Your fan clubs. Your cheerleaders and support team. You need a future reader. How do you get that?

You connect with people. You reach out. You start your author platform today even if you just wrote the first line of new WIP (Work in Progress).

You are an author, remember that. I'm bringing up Chapter 1 again to revisit you. You are no longer making excuses and are finding out what works for you. Now, you're learning all the tools at your disposal to do the work the Lord has set before you to accomplish. You don't have a blank page anymore. You are finding that with excuses removed, you can prioritize and set small goals. You can squeeze in a small amount of writing time. The tools are there. Even if they are basic, it's really all you need.

What other tools can help you accomplish your overall goals of becoming an author in the industry?

Social media will be your greatest tool.

Get ready.

I'm sending you on a quest. Grab your journal, a pen, the note section of your phone, or go ahead and start your computer. I'll wait.

Challenge:

Start building your author platform today. Here are the steps I took. I'm breaking it down to you like a checklist. Skip around if you like, but get it all going! The sooner you invest in this work the better.

First things first: What's your author name going to be? Think of an author branding name. You need this before you take any other step. Take a break. Spend time with God for Him to reveal a branding name for you. Pray about it. Talk to your family or friends.

I knew I needed a name to set my social media platforms apart. I was googling Jen Lowry and too many were popping up. I needed to add something else to my name, something that would be easy to share with others when I was out and about. A name they could connect with and could remember when they left me. Nothing fancy. Nothing outrageous or long. Something that would identify myself as an author to others and maybe stick in their minds so when they did have a chance to look me up later, they could locate me on the internet.

I researched other authors out there making it. How were they marketing themselves? What were their taglines? How did they have their websites set up? What was their Twitter handles and Instagram accounts like? Research is great, but at the end of the day, you've got to be you.

Being AUTHENTIC to you is the best advice I can give you ever.

In everything about this work from chapter one to the end of time, be you.

I prayed about it and knew the name was going to be the one that would work. The Holy Spirit gave me my business name driving down the interstate. I knew as soon as I typed in Monarch Educational Services, the name would be available. It was a God thing.

So was my author branding name. Jen Lowry Writes became the title of everything. I write. I write a lot. I write and my name is Jen Lowry. It works. For my Everyday Mom Challenge devotionals, I used Dr. Jennifer Ikner Lowry on all of my work. When it was time to build my fiction platform, I knew it needed to be separate. No YA or MG book has Dr. so and so on the cover. I didn't want it to say Jennifer – my Aunt calls me Jen, and so does my husband. It's short on the cover and it fits well. Jen Lowry. I'll do that. I write. I'll do that, too. Jen Lowry Writes was born. That's my author branding name. It's here to stay. It's what I build my author business around. You need a name. One that works for you.

1. Once you get the name, open up a Google account in that name.

This separates your author career from your personal accounts. You need to keep it separated. This is a brand, a business, and a face of your work. It's not your personal email that you do your online shopping or pay bills with. It's not your school email. It's your author email. It's your author account.

As you can guess, you can email me at jenlowrywrites@gmail.com, which is pretty cool because once someone recognizes my podcast title or my social media handles, they can easily reach out to me on email. It makes it easier for the reader. It's also easier for me. I'm not jenlowywrites24353breaker1-9. When I attempted to sign up for my Google account, it needed to be clear and easy. If you are having trouble getting a short and sweet version and it's giving you a long string of numbers or ridiculous afterthought letters/number combinations because your name is very similar to another user, rethink your platform name.

When I tried jenlowrywrites to open up my account on Google, it worked! It was easy because the name was right. Get your name ready and dive in. It's what you'll be known for. It'll all start coming together. Sign up now.

Here are the benefits of starting with Google first. You need an email address to set up author accounts on all social media platforms. You need to streamline everything. Starting with Google makes sense. Try out your platform name in Google. Here's what you'll get:

a. A personalized author email address that's easy to remember
b. Google Drive access to docs, folders, sheets for sales reports and contacts, etc.
c. Google Calendar access
d. All social media author accounts connect to this Google account
e. A YouTube account
f. Google Duo
g. Google Hangouts
h. Google Photos
i. Google Classroom
j. MORE than I'm naming here!

Now that you've got an email address, what next? Okay, more lists are coming your way. The challenge is to get every single one of the following social media sites I'm suggesting. Don't pick and choose. Do them all. Spend a day building all of your accounts. You can decorate them pretty later. I'll talk about that in another chapter. I won't leave you hanging. I've got you.

Here are the social media accounts you need to build your author platform and expand your writing community. There could be a million other ones out there I don't know, but that's where you step in and research and take control. I'm starting you off with the basics. Follow me on all of my sites if you want to see how I'm working this life. I'm not saying they're perfect. I don't have a social media manager, but I do have the time to invest in daily social media interactions. Here's my list. I challenge you to get started with each one. Go!

1. Website: I use GoDaddy because my domain name was cheaper there, but there are tons of great website developers out there that have easy to use sites, such as Weebly, Wix, WordPress, etc. www.jenlowrywrites.com[1]
2. Twitter https://twitter.com/jenlowrywrites
3. Instagram https://www.instagram.com/jenlowrywrites/

---

1. http://www.jenlowrywrites.com

4. Facebook Author Page (Start a new page under your personal page so you can easily navigate it.) https://www.facebook.com/jenlowrywrites/
5. LinkedIn https://www.linkedin.com/in/jenlowrywrites/
6. Pinterest https://www.pinterest.com/jenlowrywrites/
7. Blog: WordPress is what I use but there are others out there -https://jenlowrywrites.wordpress.com/)
8. Goodreads: https://www.goodreads.com/book/show/44306910-sweet-potato-jones
9. Patreon: https://www.patreon.com/JenLowry
10. An author podcast: I use the anchor platform because it's easy and free, but you can research others and find what's right for you! https://anchor.fm/jen-lowry-writes
11. Snapchat was recommended by some authors, but I don't use this one.
12. Tumblr – I have this and share my Instagram posts on there, but never get on the site.

Whew! That might look like a long list, but it takes just a few minutes to open each account and verify everything. Get it all going. Let it sit there today. Celebrate yourself. Yep! My idea of celebrating is grabbing a #1 from McDonalds. A health coach and author friend, Pooja Chilukuri, is probably shaking her head at me right now when she saw I listed McDonald's as my celebration reward. Sorry, just being honest. I did break the soda kick because of her.

Do your thing! Hooray! You've got an author platform. You might have zero followers today...but just wait. It's coming.

JOURNAL REFLECTION:

What was your experience building your author platform? Which social media accounts have you successfully managed in the past? How can you learn how other authors are utilizing social media? Write down short term and long-term goals for social media and your author platform. How will you celebrate your accomplishments so far? Take a picture of your celebration and mark it as a day to praise!

Just remember why you're doing all of this work. First, you're doing it for the Lord, to share the love He bestowed to you, to others. It's to edify and lift others up and encourage them. You might be the only person of faith they know or see. Make your interactions count. Be positive. Be the light.

You can't gain a follower at all if you don't have the accounts available. You must focus your attention on this work. No excuses. If you say, "But I have an aversion to social media," or "I'm not good at it," then it's a new day, folks. Let's do this right.

Let's do it for the Lord. There are tons of good that can come out of each and every one of these accounts when you use them for good and you use them to not only talk about books and the author journey, but to spread the Word of the Lord. You're building your author platform and expanding your reach. That means you are working the fields and are a laborer for the Lord in a world that needs more of Jesus.

Don't shy away from social media any longer. Embrace that it's a part of the writing career and move steps forward in the direction of learning how to manage it effectively. So many authors ask me about getting starting, and what should they do first. Well, write that novel AND build that platform simultaneously.

I say it so many times that it led me to make sure I dedicated a whole chapter on this adventure. Yes, it's an adventure. Yes, it takes a little time. But it's all worth it.

We'll get to that on the next chapter.

Right now, I still want you celebrating that you have a platform!

You've got an author platform.

You are an author.

You aren't making excuses.

You've got the blank page with SOMETHING on it.

You've got the tools you need to get started.

You've celebrated your milestones.

We're just in chapter four, and look at all of this you've accomplished. Setting those goals and crossing them off one by one...you're making progress. You're taking control. I'm very proud of you! Tag me on Twitter celebrating your author platform creation! Let me know you're reading this book and would like to connect online! I'll follow your platform! Reach out! @jenlowrywrites[2]

"And whatsoever ye do, do it heartily, as to the Lord, and not unto men; Knowing that of the Lord ye shall receive the reward of the inheritance: for ye serve the Lord Christ." Colossians 3:23-24

Pursuing Daily

Guiding Bible Verse: *"And whatsoever ye do, do it heartily, as to the Lord, and not unto men; Knowing that of the Lord ye shall receive the reward of the inheritance: for ye serve the Lord Christ." Colossians 3:23-24*

SO, NOW THAT WE'VE brought up the daily time clock, let's go ahead and discuss goal setting, time management, and planning. Oh, boy – if I could just stop you from running away from this chapter, I would. This is a must in the balance of life, and like before, no magic formula, only trial and error.

We all have busy lives in one form or fashion. We might not have the same schedules when we stack them side by side, but I wouldn't be surprised if all of us that are sharing in this devotional together have a pretty tight one filled with one activity, task, or responsibility after the other.

So, where does writing fit in? How can it even possibly work in the busy life I have?

These are great questions, not excuses at this point because we are beyond making those. It's a practical issue that many writers face, so by me saying that at least you know you aren't alone in this quandary.

Writing is a daily practice. It's a work that needs to somehow fit into the routine in our life because it's our calling, our gift from the Lord, and we need to exercise it. Funny I should mention exercise.

Let's talk moving those writing muscles. If I listed out all of my duties of the day, you'd probably shake your head and say, "Wow."

Worn.

Out.

Woman.

Sure, I'm running on fumes many days and have a couple of cups of coffee at my disposal to try to make the caffeine push into a creative space. I also know that my writing is important.

There. I said it. I find value in my writing. When you find something of importance and value (I'm using repetitive language here so that I can get you to see that your work also has importance and value), you make time for those things.

If you find your health to be important, you'll take time to research, practice new habits, and stay committed to your best healthy self. If you find spirituality to be important, you'll take time to study God's word, pray and form new habits of living, and stay committed to your beliefs. If you take your writing seriously and understand the wealth of health, happiness, and peace it will bring you, then you'll take time to research, practice daily writing in some form or fashion, and stay committed to the writing life because you write because you have to, not because you feel like it.

There are many things I don't feel like doing. Between us, if you gave me the choice of pajamas or clothes, I'm choosing pajamas every time. That also means I would prefer staying at home than going out. That also means I would rather be writing than doing any social activity. I make choices. I stand behind my choices.

I love God. I raise my family. I work to pay my bills. I write because I must.

When you realize that writing is important and it brings value to your life, the shift begins to happen. It might not be like tectonic plates shifting underneath your feet, and you might not even begin to feel the change in the atmosphere at first. Or it might hit you full force and you dive in. The point is, change will come when you prioritize. Blank pages will be swallowed up whole. Chapters will be written. Edits will be done. A book will manifest, and you'll say, "Wow."

Wonderful.
Oh, how,
Wonderful.

There's an old-timey gospel hymn that comes to mind when I read that over again. There's nothing like finishing that first page, chapter, and novel. There's nothing like receiving your first box of books in the mail and holding a book party reveal in your very own home (preferably in pajamas). There's nothing like seeing your work in your hands and out of your heart and mind. But to get to that point, the work has to be done. Period.

We will always be a work in progress, but we will always have to progress to get the work completed. How can we do that?

We schedule time. We find time in our day. We figure out when our best times are to write, and they are different for everyone I talk to. I love to listen to authors share their journey and their process. That's a highlight of my Jen Lowry Writes podcast, interviewing others about their own author life.

When the Lord opened the door for me to interview Kate DiCamillo, she gave us the insider track on her daily routine. You can listen on the podcast or head over to my YouTube channel to watch our video together and see me all cheesing: https://www.youtube.com/watch?v=LqsJUAdSYQQ&t=2222s

5 am wakeup to the smell of coffee brewing.
Write two pages. Leave it alone.
Journal.
Read a book.
Journal.
Read a book.
The next day do it all over again.

Her routine is not my routine, but it works for her, as we all know. Anyone that's picked up a Kate book knows she's got it going on in the kid lit realm. She writes with heart, hope, and healing. She's my favorite children's literature author, hands down (more about that later). Anyway, before I get on a tangent about how much I love children's literature, I want you to get back to thinking about two pages.

I bet you are a little stunned to hear that two pages is the productivity level of such an AMAZING writer, and wonder how in the world could you ever get anything done with just two pages. I'm not a math person, but I'm telling you guys, I pulled out my phone calculator later that evening and thought that thing through.

2 pages x 365 days a year = 730 pages

Now, two typed pages is a crazy large amount when you consider that most books are 5x8 – 6x9, so with margin readjustments, you are talking WAY more in your actual book page count conversion.

There we have it. An answer to what a minimum should be in our daily routine. If you completed two pages a day, think of the work you could get accomplished. Even one page a day! Seriously, y'all. WE CAN DO THIS!

I'm still speaking this over my life, too. Everything I'm saying to you in this devotional, I'm living it and continuing to challenge myself to do. Just because I have bestsellers out there doesn't mean I stop. It means I have to keep up the momentum, continue to write and read, connect on social media, and all the necessary business stuff that comes along with the author life (more on that later). I want to improve, to learn, and to continue to increase my reach.

I want to share my routine with you on how my life looks just in case you still think you can't fit the time

Daily podcast at 6:00 am.

Full-time job beginning at 6:55 am – 2:18 pm

Afternoon nap or writing or reading or scheduled podcast interviews.

Dinner. (Some days I have help from my son and husband, other days I'm putting it all together. I plan the days out in advance, including two crock pot meals each week I have a recipe page on Pinterest: https://www.pinterest.com/jenlowrywrites/)

Homeschool until 10:00 pm

Writing, reading, watching a documentary or snoring on the couch.

During the week, that doesn't look like I get a lot of writing in. In fact, there might be a day or two that I don't get a chance to write or edit a WIP. I might focus on other writing tasks like social media blasts, a blog posts or a poem. You see I used "or" a few times because it's just according to the day what I need to recharge. It might be a middle grades book or the day may lend itself more to a nap. I might have a spark of inspiration and need thirty sustained minutes to write or I might watch a documentary instead.

I also found what gets the greatest hits for me. I get tons of views when I put up a poem I write from the point of view of my characters, or just a poem on whatever it is struck me to inspire me to write it. I also get hits on tutorials and tips. My podcast interviews draw in the crowds, and I get more hits on Facebook Live than YouTube. How do I know all of this so fast off the fingertips? Because I do the "or" and figure things out. I keep it fresh. I'm circulating and moving around the writing routine.

My weekend looks completely different. We do have homeschool Saturday adventures together each week, and yes, that's what we call them. But I'm up by 5:30 am cranking out some serious writing time. It's my time to study the Word, get to going on writing goals, and nonstop typing action begins. It's like I bottle it all up during the week to make it to my early Saturday and Sunday morning routines.

I will write most Saturdays until UFC hits the prelim time. That's my reward, watching fights with my son. So, it's early to rise and momma catching words instead of worms, and then we're off to explore the world together as family. I come home and settle back in (with pajamas) and write, write, write until the fights come on. Again. It's my routine. It works for me.

On Sundays, it's the same 5:30 am rise up with the Word and the words God gives me to write for the day. I'm off to church and then the grocery store, and back to writing until supper. Afterwards, I'm back at it again. It's my weekend warrior writing boot camp routine. You should've seen my summer.

I wasn't homeschooling or working at the high school over the summer break, so imagine my day filled with nothing but a laptop, pajamas, and words. It was fabulous and very productive. The books flowed because I created a safe space for them to breathe and live. They welcomed me each morning and each day was a new twist and turn and character reveal. It was fascinating to see how the work kept coming. There was no time to waste. The books were banked, and now I have a list online to prove that sustained writing time can produce fruit. I'm living that bestselling author dream right now because my summer routine consisted of daily goal setting.

But it wasn't just the summer. I started writing *A Magical Christmas Wedding* (187 pages) with my full-time job schedule and released it on October 24, 2019. It took me a full three months to write it with a weekend writing warrior schedule and some work nights built in to edit. It is possible. It's hard, but it's possible. I cried when I finished that book. Not just because I wrote it in memory of my momma, but because it was something I accomplished while living the hectic life. Happy tears. Exhausted, but happy tears. Worth it tears.

You've got to find out what works for you.

Your writing is important.

Your writing is valuable.

It is not a hobby. There, I said it. It's a calling from God. He has called you for this purpose. I spent years praying to the Lord, wondering what "my purpose" was and how could I best serve Him. He showed me this past year the fullness of being an author that serves Him first, and then the reader.

My author career is all for the Lord and from the Lord.

Repeat that line.

My author career is all for the Lord and from the Lord.

It doesn't come from any other place. It's not based on how smart you are, how gifted you are in grammar and style, or how much education or experience you have. It's all about Jesus. Think of Luke. Yeah, Luke, the great physician. He was also a great author. He had a full-time job, but his calling was to spread the message of Christ and the works of the Apostles.

Luke was divinely appointed by the Lord to do this work, and he has such beloved books of the Bible. His work was anointed.

We are also divinely appointed as Christians to carry out the calling God gifts us with to do His work while we can. Think of your writing as a way you can give back your heart and time and energy to serve the Lord, as a Christian missionary from your very fingertips to a laptop to the world. You can inspire others, encourage them, lift them up, bring them hope, show a different way, promote friendship, relationships, love, joy, and entertain others by providing them an escape from the harsh realities of the world into the hands of a book that you wrote to give back to the Lord.

I shared this Bible verse with a dear friend to encourage her. When I share out the Word, I call them "Soul Stickers," and she found great comfort in it. I sent her the image and she kept it on her phone. She told me she'd never heard the particular verse before but it was a powerful reminder to her about who she's working for.

This is a wonderful verse you need to meditate on day and night until it plants the seeds in you to do this work for the One who called you to it in the first place.

"And whatsoever ye do, do it heartily, as to the Lord, and not unto men; Knowing that of the Lord ye shall receive the reward of the inheritance: for ye serve the Lord Christ." Colossians 3:23-24

Maybe then it won't seem daunting. Maybe then it won't seem overwhelming in the midst of your everyday. Maybe then you'll see that when you do this writing life "heartily" with joy for the Lord, freedom will begin to live within the space between your heart and the screen and you'll create goals, try them out, and readjust to meet the needs of your time.

Frustration won't live where that hope lives. Giving up won't be allowed where that knowledge manifests. You will preserver, and you will write. Because you'll realize that your writing is important and of value. You'll know. You'll change. You'll write.

And when you know what you know...there's no stopping that. Get ready!

But when we discuss time and routines, we also have to discuss the dangers of chasing rabbit holes. Lord help us all when we get distracted. What can we do to bring ourselves back once the time starts clicking away and we find ourselves spending more time on one area when we should be focused on the writing before us?

Since we are talking about the never-ending rabbit holes that can take us away from the actual writing process, take heed of the proverb by Confucius, "The man who chases two rabbits catches neither." There is wisdom in this.

JOURNAL REFLECTION: How can this proverb translate over into our writing life? How can chasing two rabbits at once, when we are well meaning and have good intentions, take us away from our final product?

THERE IS A BIBLE VERSE that also applies to distraction as well. Satan will step into the picture to steal your time, energy, creative flow, and productivity. Why? Because he doesn't want the work you are producing to get into the hands of readers. That's the bottom line of it. You can call it human interaction, but I call it forces that are trying to steal, kill, and destroy your joy and your passion for writing so a reader doesn't have a chance to hear your message. He doesn't want you to encourage others or spread the love of Jesus. He wants to hinder and halt the divine appointment that's on your life. That means distractions, even the simplest of these, can be removed from your sight and mind by rebuking Satan.

"The thief comes only to steal and kill and destroy; I have come that they may have life, and have it to the full." John 10:10

When you face challenges in this author life, remember that there is an enemy lurking to deter God's children from the truth and the way. Paul was clear to the converts at Thessalonica who was causing the stumbling block, *"For we wanted to come to you—certainly I, Paul, did, again and again—but Satan blocked our way." I Thessalonians 2:18*

But the letter still arrived. The message was still spread. The word could not be withheld and didn't find itself in a void When you get distracted, remember who you are writing for. If you start getting distracted, lose your way, or get discouraged, push the anxiety or fears away with repeating this verse,

"Jesus turned and said to Peter, "Get behind me, Satan! You are a stumbling block to me; you do not have in mind the concerns of God, but merely human concerns." Matthew 16:23

This writing time you are devoting is just not for you. Even though there is strong research that suggests writing is therapeutic and wonderful for our mental health, it's also a calling. It's not for you alone, even though you do need to do this for yourself – it's a peace giving endeavor. It's not for your family, even though they can be a great inspiration. It's not even for the reader alone, even though without the reader you can't make the connection and spread the message. It's for the Lord. Period. The Lord will then provide you with all you need.

"And my God will meet all your needs according to the riches of his glory in Christ Jesus." Philippians 4:19

If you're the type of person that can get lost for hours in the world of social media and setting up your platform, then you'll need to set yourself some parameters to control the time you spend building your author community. I say this because you're also writing at the same time. You're working on honoring your blank page, too.

I am not talking smack or fussing about such distractions, I'm speaking real, and I've seen it happen. I've seen good intention writers tell me ten million other things they do other than write.

Once I was out with a friend, and she had a bundle in her hands. She looked at me and raised an eyebrow. I had nothing in my hands. I was holding it in and exhibiting self-control.

She started to debate whether or not she needed what was piled up before her. I asked her, "Do you need it?"

She answered, "No, but I want it."

"Is it useful for you?"

"No, but I want it."

"Will it bring you joy?"

She stopped and looked and me and reconsidered her purchases. She left out of the store with less, but the ones that mattered.

CHALLENGE:

The next time you start down a path when you know you should be writing, ask yourself these three questions:

1. Do you need to do it?
2. Is it useful for you?
3. Will it bring you joy?

I've talked to many published authors who tell me they struggle with time management, motivation, and routines. They also don't have the balance of social media in check and can spend hours chasing after strange polls and laughing at memes, and watching nonsense videos that go viral for some reason I can't explain. There is a time and place for all of that. How about as a celebration AFTER you've finished your writing goals for the day?

I don't want anything to stop your progress. I definitely don't want you to be standing in your own way. If you need to ask Jesus to move the mountain, it might be the mountain of your mind to be cast into the sea so that you can get out of your own way to have freedom to write. To free up your own time.

JOURNAL REFLECTION: How well do you manage time on your own? Do you have a calendar, a goal planning guide, or use some online tool to help you? Do you need monitoring or an accountability partner? Do you need a wake-up call? A literal alarm?

I don't want you binging movies, and then at the end of the night feel guilty that you didn't write. I don't want you spending two hours talking about writing on social media and twenty minutes staring at a blank page not sure of what to write. Spend the two hours talking to God if you must, and then stare at the blank page. Write, then get on social media and talk about writing. It's time to get real. Don't get distracted. Do the work set before you as if you are working for the Lord and not man.

Ask yourself this question out of the two, should social media vs. writing your book take precedent? Well, of course if you only have a limited amount of time in a day, you should devote it to writing.

So, what is the minimum? What's the balance?

What if I told you once you get your social media accounts in motion, all you need is about ten minutes to devote to social media? It's a great start and it won't evaporate your time. Try to find ten minutes somewhere in your day which could mean during a lunch break or the car line, waiting on the pasta water to boil, or the credits to roll.

I'm going to give you a warning though. If you find yourself spending way more time worrying over social media, you'll lose sight of your bigger picture – your manuscript. If you try to compare yourself to other authors and how many followers they have, it could get you discouraged. They had to start somewhere. Remember you are starting. Start. Don't compare. That's another distractor and a stealer of joy and progress if I ever saw one.

You do need to build your platform, though. Publishing companies and literary agents may ask for your social media accounts right out the gate to see what presence you have in the author community. If you self-publish, you'll need to also continue to network and grow your social media accounts because that's a way you can promote and market in the future.

I've met some pretty spectacular authors and readers through social media, and without my push to get on there regardless of my limited knowledge of how to do the mess, I show up. I'm me. I'm figuring it out as I go, and I might not know all I'm doing with it, but I'm out there. I'm showing up every single day. I'm pursuing daily, and I'm challenging you to do the same.

Social media management and writing time is a dance routine we must learn to master. You're about to step on stage, and if you fall flat on your face the first couple of spins, then you've got the ability to pick yourself right back up and figure it all out again. Don't get stuck in a rut or chase rabbits for long, your manuscript will never get done, and we don't want that, do we?

Remember there is no golden rule to this writing life but there's a way to finding out YOU. You must imagine yourself as a research experiment.

You only have so many hours in a day. You need to organize, prioritize, list, review, reflect, address, move, say no, say yes, figure it out, add shortcuts, make adjustments, and keep researching until you understand what your balance is. If you are out of balance, keep trying. Keep adding a new thing or taking away one that doesn't work for you.

You might start out with seven minutes of writing time, or you might be able to devote twenty minutes to a half day sprint. We are all different and our schedules can be off the chain crazy, so there's no way I can give you the secret key that opens a magical portal of writing wisdom of how much time you need to crank out the next bestselling book All I can say is that you need to figure out your writing routine that works best for you. This needs to happen. It needs to happen daily. Daily. Just like prayer. Daily.

CHALLENGE:

Figure out what time of day you write the best. When are you most productive? Establish a goal to either write so many minutes, pages, or word count objectives per day. Whatever you like. I just like to write until I can't anymore. I tried the whole word count per day thing and that actually drove me a little foolish having to constantly look down at the left hand of my screen to see how many words I was tackling and it turned out to stifle me and worry me. Instead, I just wrote until I couldn't. You might need the word count or day page count like Kate DiCamillo.

You might try a weekend warrior write. You can support my author life and become a part of my WWW elite team on Patreon to join my writing bootcamp routine to encourage and motivate authors. https://www.patreon.com/JenLowry You might wait for a break or time off, or an early morning or late night write. If you practice writing daily, you'll start to notice things about your writing that you might have missed before. You need a daily dedicated time, even if you do like my author friend Carol. She makes an appointment with herself to write. Your challenge is to set a goal. Carry it out. Evaluate it. Try it again if it worked, tweak it if it didn't.

JOURNAL REFLECTION:

After writing for one week, journal about your experiences. What did you notice about yourself? What were your strengths? What were roadblocks that might hinder your progress? What are ways you can get around those obstacles?

THINK CREATIVELY AND try a new way. After the next week, journal again about your writing habits you're forming. Are you making progress? What is your current writing state in comparison to the week before? Give yourself a little grace. If life happens, don't carry guilt with you. Take care of yourself, then make the writing happen when you can.

Dear Lord,

Thank you for the gift of writing. Thank you for equipping me with what I need to do the work you've set before me to do. Thank you for helping me to set goals and prioritize time. I need your help, Lord. Please guide my steps and help me to see a straight path to take in a road that has so many. Help me stay focused, determined, and dedicated to completing my book. I am doing this all to serve you, Lord, to bring you honor and glory.

Amen

Weekly Planner

"Commit to the Lord whatever you do, and he will establish your plans." Proverbs 16:3

Monday

Tuesday

Wednesday

Thursday

Friday

Saturday

Sunday

Don't Forget!

To Do:

Praise Playlist:

And whatever
you do, whether
in word or deed,
do it all in the
name of the Lord
Jesus, giving
thanks to God the
Father
through him.
Colossians 3:17

Of All the Things I Could be Doing

Guiding Bible Verse: *"And whatever you do, whether in word or deed, do it all in the name of the Lord Jesus, giving thanks to God the Father through him."*
Colossians 3:17

Of all the things I could be doing, I'd rather be praising Jesus while I'm writing or reading. You know my schedule, so I'm going to share with you how I fit my reading time in. I call it research. I'm definitely reading for pleasure and just for the love of it, but when I can convince my brain that it's for *the cause,* then I'm more likely to advance to the book stash and dive in.

Yes, I have a stash. Not a shelf. I'm working on that issue now. I'm giving my husband the eye – the one that asks, could you please build me a bookshelf? In the meantime, I have books hidden all through the house. Don't tell him to look in the ottoman or under my shoes in the closet. And I won't even begin to show you the picture of my office at work and the ginormous bookshelf I have there filled with layers upon layers of books!

Okay, you caught me. I've got a book love that I can't deny. It's been with me since my earliest memories.

Of all the things I could be doing, I'd rather be writing or reading. So, what do I read? The Word of the Lord is first and foremost what we all should be reading. The Bible is our weapon against the enemy. It is our strength and our comforter. We have the Word for us as an instructional manual.

"I remember the days of old; I meditate on all that you have done; I ponder the work of your hands." Psalm 143:5

When we remind ourselves that the people of the Bible were just that – real life, flesh and blood, breathing, walking people, just like us, it can give us a comfort beyond anything imaginable when we reflect on how God sustained then and now. He is our ever-constant presence, and His eye is on us. Amen and Amen for that, double Amens are needed.

How could we expect to work through our daily lives without a dependency upon God and His Word? How could we ever get through driver's education without a manual and a steady guide to make us do crazy hand gestures at stop signs to prove I was actually stopping the car (apparently, I would do some roll technique he didn't approve of)? How do we think we can do this all on our own and go through life without reading the Bible? I don't know how it could be possible, and I don't ever want to find out. So, that's my first reading and one that I will challenge you to take if you don't have time for any other book in the day! The Word must be planted in our heart. Trust me, it will CHANGE YOUR LIFE! So, if that's the start you need, fill your life with the Word, and then we can talk about book studies later. In the meantime, remember the purpose of the Word:

"Thy word is a lamp unto my feet, and a light unto my path." Psalm 119:105

Besides the Bible there are some great author career books out there you can research. I think I need to mention this because I know other writers who depend on these author self-help tools to keep them on the right path with story structure, dialogue, and character development. There are some top-notch ones out there in the industry and can be found on bestseller lists and author recommendations for author craft books on their blogs or podcasts.

Yes, there are long lists of these. But they aren't necessarily on my list. A writing community I'm involved with just finished a book study on the *Save the Cat* series by Blake Snyder or Jessica Brody and found it tremendously helpful. There are tons of these bestselling books that are circulating to help with plot formation, identifying themes, how to create stellar dialogue, so on and so forth.

So, if you're at this point in your life where you feel like studying author craft books could help you get an edge on story development, look for those specifically that would address your genre or style, but at the end of the day, always remember you've got to honor the blank page. The page will speak for itself. Once your characters start talking, they'll knock until you answer and pound your brain until you place them on a page, giving them a place to reside.

If you need research books about the art of writing, go for it! I encourage you to do it. Google the top ten list of recommended books for authors. Check them out at your local library or buy your copy to annotate and sticky note the mess out of it. Authors I know are always looking for book study of worthy author craft books. The lists are out there and they'd be easy to discover.

Go for it. If that's what you need. If not, stick around for another strategy for reading for research I actually began in 2020 and my lightbulb came on! Epiphany central.

Of all the things I'd rather be praising Jesus while writing and reading. So, what do I read if I don't read author craft self-help books? I'm glad you asked!

I read in my genre I'm interested in writing about and the target population of who I'm interested in writing for.

Once I opened myself up to the blank page, to honor it and give myself a shove out of the way to let the work come, the Lord has taken me to multiple genres I'd never thought I would explore. He's opened up a wide door for me, and all I have to do is accept the call to walk on in. It's a warm beckoning to learn as I go.

I love that about this author life. Who is a know-it-all in life anyway? And if you know one, I bet the image alone of the person might make you twitch your lip. No one is perfect at this, not even those with a Pulitzer Prize award for literature. We are all learning as we go.

Stay open to learning and trying new things. One day, you'll have an epiphany while reading, too. It's probably already happened to you, and I'm just late to the game. Let me tell you the story of how mine came to be.

Oh, can I tell you a shame-on-me fallacy I once believed. I actually thought I should stay away from reading earlier on when I wanted to chase this author life, because I was too afraid. I was scared I would fall into the trap of reading a book and then somehow getting too close to it, like I would lift the pages and they become mine. Oh, foolish me. On the contrary, I needed to be reading *veraciously*, like a lion devouring every living book on the plain to survive.

I needed to be reading like my life depended on it.

Now that I get it, I want you to get it. I want to convince you of something so I'm doing the lean in. Lean in with me. Pay close attention to this one because it's a great tip that will truly make you a better writer. You'll see just after one month of doing this. I have full confidence in this strategy.

Just like your work is important and just like your work is of value, there are notable works in every genre that are important, valued, and well-loved. How do you know they're loved and appreciated? If you are into children's literature as much as me, you'll recognize gold or silver stampings on books for notable contributions in the field. They might have a gold stamp on them that says The John Newberry Medal which recognizes and praises memorable, long lasting works in children's literature.

They may be on the New York Times or USA Bestsellers list. They might have a movie out, and if you're like me, you want to get your hands on that so you can have movie night and play the comparison game.

Find books that are circulating and matter to the mass population. Get copies of those books. Study them.

If they have a bestselling stamp beside their book, it might be worthy to consider reading them because that also means people are buzzing about them. It's all the rave. You can readily find reviews of these books and read testimonials. Authors will possibly have a large social media presence, and you can listen to their author interviews.

The books that are circulating on lists and book clubs and social media frenzy reports are essential for us to know about within the genre that we're writing. Movies are being made from them. It's worthy of your time to invest learning what makes those books special, standout, and all around fabulous.

It's also more than just the research of what makes those works stand out in the market, but it's also for comparable title lists that you need to build to show where your book concept fits within the market. This is very important when you are talking with booksellers, agents, or the general public about your book. If you know widely popular books, you're most likely to get a recognizable nod and a stronger connection could be made between you and the person you've approached about your own book.

I'm giving you a pause here to decide which way you want to go with your next challenge. Read Challenge A and B, and then decide! Alter your book list based after you pray about this decision. It's how you spend your time researching that could really boost your writing, connections, and communication about books. This must become part of your story. Decide if it's A or B. Or you can do both and alternate. There's no perfect plan. You just need to create your own routine. Try one and hop to the other if you find it's not an effective use of your time. See how flexible this challenge can be! Work it out! Start reading! Today!

Challenge A:

You're not ready to hold an intensive book study in your genre of interest yet, but would like to stick to author craft self-help books. Make a list of the top ten books. Order them through interlibrary loan at your public library or get your own copy. Have fun breaking each book apart! A guide sheet on how to get started with a book study is included at the end of this chapter.

Challenge B:

You're ready to dive right into books within your genre and target population. Create a list of the top ten notable books in your specific area and start your search for the books today. Don't delay! This can be a powerful move for you in your author career. Not only will you see an improvement in your writing, but in the way you "talk books" with others.

Since I'm working with **Challenge B** in 2019-2020, I want to share with you the process I went to and how I even fell into this idea to begin with. Was it all by chance? No way. I believe this was a divine appointment the Lord had for me, and I'm glad I showed up. It's changing my understanding of the craft and planting seeds!

When I found out that Kate DiCamillo, the real Kate, was to appear on my podcast, I knew I had to dive in to her collection. I LOVE her books. She's my favorite author. Take a journey with her different books but one thing remains the same. That lady has a heart that beats inside of a book, and it cycles hurting to hopeful. I also love she writes for a wide age range in the children's and juvenile book market.

Anyway, I needed to prepare for the upcoming podcast interview so I had to read *Beverly, Right Here*, but before I could get to that I had to start with *Raymie Nightingale*. One book led to the next book, led to me picking up every Kate book on the library shelf. Now, I have a collection of Kate's work. Each one has a very special place in my heart. They are books that matter.

But it also mattered when I started to see more than just the words. The patterns started emerging. I became an investigator of the word. I knew there was something strong in this line of work, to research authors who are well loved, and Kate is well loved by MANY. Just look at her two Newberry medals, movies, countless fans, etc. If you ask anyone, "Have you heard of Because of Winn-Dixie or The Tale of Despereaux," many will squeal with delightful recognition.

After I went through a month of Kate dedicated books, I knew I needed to continue this work. So, how did I start? I realized that my happy place in writing was middle grades and children's literature. The Raptor Revolution was the most fun I've had writing a book. It's Sam's (my 12-year-old) favorite, so I knew I wanted to focus on middle grades and children's literature in 2020.

I settled in with a genre list from bestselling authors who have had a long career in the industry. I went on a genre hunt and created a list of authors who I wanted to study. Since I'm currently reading the Harry Potter series in our homeschool and last year, I read the Percy Jackson series, I knew I needed to find other wildly popular books.

So, where do I go for advice? My kid! He's in the range of the target population I'm going for, so I had him to list out his favorite children's movies. *Matilda* and *James and the Giant Peach* popped up in the conversation so Roald Dahl became the next on my list for an author study.

I didn't want to do this work alone because I value conversation around books. Besides, the whole point of me doing an author study is to break apart what's working. I felt like it would be beneficial to start a weekly author book club to investigate this work and learn from other authors as well. What were they noticing? What did they find surprising? When I can talk out books with others, I can also include what they learn through the author study, because in that way, I could advance my own development and understanding.

I approached an online community and asked would they be interested in an author book study. One lady stepped up and it's been fabulous! I've grown so much in this venture. I have a research purpose. I have a schedule and an accountability partner. We've read two books by Roald Dahl and are now working on *Charlie and the Chocolate Factory* as the last of his work and will move on to E.B. White.

Weekly book talks have been amazing for my own author development. I come to the talk with a notebook and write constant notes! The author study has been so helpful, I'm setting it as a goal for 2020. My librarians found out what I was up to and started giving me a long list of recommended authors. "If you love Kate, then you'll love..." and the list keeps growing.

So, what could be a good start for you?

Look for the top ten in your genre, find author's with multiple titles that are widely known (award winning, movie versions, etc.) and start to read. The more an author is widely known, you can connect with a reader base out there. Even if they may never buy your book, you can share a great conversation about books you love. A deeper connection is made. Know your genre. Know the stories that matter in it.

We evaluate. We read with an author lens. We break it apart. We notice things we've never thought of before, like patterns, word choice, freedom of language, risks – and we realize we have hit the jackpot with research.

We need to live within our own genres and improve our own craft. I'm giving you permission right now to read children's books, if that's where your heart is navigating you toward. I'm giving you permission to read suspense, mystery or horror, if that's the place you want to plant your seeds and grow a garden. Find your place. Live there. Grow.

Reasons why we should read top rated books within our genre:

1. It can help us connect our books to comparable titles. Publishing companies want to know where you book would stack up beside on a shelf and what it's most like out there within the last five years. If you can't answer that question, you need to rectify that now. It's not lesser known authors at this point. You need to read the high-profile authors because that's who the literary agents will recognize. They won't recognize my name, Jen Lowry (not yet, anyway). If you say Stephen King, they recognize it. If you say Rick Riordan or J.K. Rowling, they know it.

2. It can open doors for communicating with others about books in general. We need to be able to talk books. Not just about our books, but about books that move us and inspire us. Books that change our lives. But not just books that are wide in every genre, but books that sit within the shelves of our own work. When we start talking to others about popular books, that's an in for you to talk about your own work, too.

3. We need to see what works. The more you stick within your genre; I guarantee you'll become a stronger editor of your own work. You can step back into your manuscript with a fresher vision of how to make your work a cleaner version of its once messy self. Noticing the little nuisances, you might frequently make that need to be removed can come from actually reading in your genre. I cut out 12,000 words of unnecessary words after reading Kate's work in a month. Look at the

difference that makes to the total story flow! Without my research, I may not have edited my manuscript in this way.

4. We need to love our own genre if we're writing in it. That should be where we want to live. The reading wide concept is great. I applaud people who do that. But when I have a limited amount of time to give to any given tasks because of my life schedule, I have to be very selective of what I read. That means don't hand me an adult fiction read any time soon. I feel called to write in the middle grades/easy reader chapter book, picture book target population. That's where I'm living and completely filled with joy!

5. An author study is one of the most valuable endeavors you'll undertake. Choose an author in your genre that's had enormous success. I learned this through a divine appointment. I picked up Kate DiCamillo and went through almost all of her books (still working on it – this is a goal), and not only did she become my favorite children's literature author, but I learned so much about writing.

6. Grab an author that writes series work in your genre. You can catch on to the little intricacies that make hearts tick. Investigate the top author's works that have made a lasting career out of writing.

7. Grab a friend to read with you. I love my weekly online video chat on Zoom (free) with another children's lit author. We started our own book club and are in the world of Roald Dahl now.

CHALLENGE:

Whether you read author craft or genre work, create a reading goal today. Goodreads can help you track it. I also have a Pinterest board where I pin the books I've read. I started off the year with picking 70 as my goal, just because my favorite number is seven, and I needed more than that! I will say that I've exceeded my goal for the year because I've also included picture books in the total count.

JOURNAL REFLECTION:

What books make you happy? Make a list of your top ten books. This would be great to document in a blog and on social media. Who are your favorite authors? See if there are any interviews of them on YouTube or online. What can you learn from them? What genre do you think you'll write in? Will you write in multiple areas or focus on one? What have you learned about your writing so far?

God is within her she will not fall; God will help her at break of day.
Psalm 46:5

Good Enough

Guiding Bible Verse: *"God is within her she will not fall; God will help her at break of day." Psalm 46:5*

SOMETIMES I HAVE TO admit, I'm my own worst enemy. I can get down on myself super quick. You wouldn't think about me if you knew me. People often describe me as being optimistic, happy all of the time, and ready to step in to help. I carry the smile.

But when it's just me, alone, my heart can race with worry I've built up over this one question that can plague me at the worst and even best of times:

Am I good enough? Will my writing be well received and liked? Will I even get a review, and when I do, will it be a good one?

When I gathered the courage to put my writing as a top priority over the summer and give it all to the Lord, I found the words trickle out from my fingertips without stopping. One book turned into two and then more and more. How was this happening? I only can give credit to the Holy Spirit because I'm just not that smart. I'm not that good, but God is.

People would doubt it. They'd ask, "How can you do that?" I heard, "There's no way you wrote all those books," to "I bet you self-published," like there was a black cloud over the whole work I dedicated to the Lord and my family. Like it wasn't good enough.

I made the choice to grow my author business. I wanted to step out in faith and do what I felt called to do. The nagging voice still remained, and this time, with the outside influence of naysayers:

Am I good enough? Will I ever be enough? Will my contributions be enough?

This book is not to go into all the reasons why you should self-publish, traditionally publish, or become a hybrid published author (like me). I don't want to even begin to go into this discussion with you because I don't want you to get overwhelmed with all of the different avenues you can take in this new publishing age.

Right now, it's about you believing in YOU, that you have a story to tell, so tell it. We all have a story. I've met so many wonderful people in my life and each and every one of them has a story to tell. They might not be meant to step into this author world because their calling may be in another gifted area from the Lord, but they still have a story.

You are reading this book because you know this is your spiritual calling. The Lord is not letting you go astray. He's got you right where you need to be, to develop and grow, to learn and to explore and research, and to embrace the fact that you're good enough for what he's called you to do.

If you want to read an inspirational story about overcoming challenges and obstacles, stumbling through excuses, and then following the will of God, just go straight to the Word of God and follow the life of Moses. Read this quick snapshot.

"Moses said to the LORD, 'Pardon your servant, Lord. I have never been eloquent, neither in the past nor since you have spoken to your servant. I am slow of speech and tongue.'" Exodus 4:10

Moses doubted before going to Pharaoh. Can you imagine the great fear that fell upon him? The Lord had plans to use Moses, and that He did. The Lord has plan for you, and if you're reading this book, I am sure of it – you have a purpose and a story. You have your own unique experience, and want to share it out. You just need the belief and the faith to see it through.

It's scary. I know it. I was scared once, too. But I'm so thankful I stopped running from God and from the stories welling up within me. I'm so grateful the Lord chose me for this work, and I'm glad He chose you, too.

It's a humbling experience to realize you've been called into the work of the Lord, to use the story God has given you to reach others. You are special. He has plans for you.

"'For I know the plans I have for you' declares the Lord, 'Plans to prosper you and not to harm you, plans to give you hope and a future.'" Jeremiah 29:11

Journal Reflection: Meditate on the Word of the Lord. What verses is He leading you to read? If you want to stay on Jeremiah 29:11, live there in these next moments and pray to the Lord with thankfulness. Thank you, God, for choosing me to become an author and share my story. Thank you in advance on how you will use me and my story to touch the lives of others. I may not know the ending, but I know you do, and it's to help me prosper, not to harm me. It's to give me a hope and a future. Thank you for your gifts. Amen.

I was recently asked by someone who's interested in writing a book, "Do you think anyone would want to even read it?"

The answer is YES. My response is, "Do you know how many people are currently in the world?"

There is one out there who needs your story to be told or your heart wouldn't be yearning to do this work. This work is not about you. It can help you. It can heal you. It can be so rewarding for you. However, it's not about you at all. There's one. Waiting.

Here's the bottom line. If you ask this question of whether or not you have a story worth sharing or have this nagging doubt in your mind still, we need to have a "come to Jesus" meeting.

We've made it midway through the book. Facts are that doubt can creep in at any time. You've got to put on the whole armor of God when the attacks start to come your way so you can battle the urge to quit. Guess who wins when you quit? The devil. Because that means your story can't reach that one person who needs it.

Don't let the devil win. Don't let him steal your joy. Being an author is a great joy. It has its ups and downs like anything else in life, but it's worth the journey. It's all worth it. Trust me.

Writing a book is not just so you can become the next big thing in the market. It's not even about making a bestseller list, even though it's nice when you do. Don't get me wrong. Anyone that puts their time, energy, and efforts into any process wants a return on investment. If you walk in only waiting for the paycheck or the accolades or the shout outs, that's when you might just set yourself up for disappointment.

How about if you walked into this with your heart and eyes wide open. This will give you a better perspective, and when challenges come, and they will, you'll have an intrinsic motivation that can help inspire you to keep moving forward.

It will come from that internal spring of hope, not an external force or reason to keep you pushing on.

What if I told you when you become an author and do publish your book, regardless of whatever route you take, you're ending up at the same place. You'll be on a shelf, whether brick and mortar or digital, to reach one person.

Just one?

Yes, just one. Go into this author career with this attitude, and you'll be humbled and grateful for each and every connection you make. Even if that just one is you.

Be happy with just one. If you walk in with the mentality that you're writing for millions, you'll get disappointed if you don't sell millions. If you are writing your story because it matters, then it will matter, and you'll fill the joy overwhelm and spill over when you receive your first box of books in the mail with your name on the cover. Even if it's just for one.

One touches thousands.

Here's what I mean by this. Let's say you have a story you want to tell. You don't know how it's all going to end at this moment, but you've got a pretty idea. You know this book matters. The themes are powerful. The message is strong. It needs to be told.

Write for Jesus, first.

Write for you, because you must.

Write for one reader.

Not millions. Write for one reader.

If your book sales one copy, praise Jesus.

How many people does that one person have around them? How many people can they go out and encourage and share the message? They may know thousands. They may know one. One more. The seeds could be planted in that one person for change.

Yes, reading can do that. It can make someone more compassionate and caring, more thoughtful, or understanding. It can broaden a perspective. It can make someone think in new ways. Books are a powerful mediator, and it can start with just one reader. If books didn't have that profound influence on us, we wouldn't be authors to begin with. We know it matters.

So, why do we tell ourselves our stories are different? Like we don't matter. Oh, we do. We do. We matter to Jesus. This is our missionary calling. Serve the

Lord and by doing so, you'll be enough. Come even with your weaknesses, and know God will get you through it. Weakness in an area doesn't mean you aren't good enough. It just means you have lots to learn in an area or two or three. Embrace the not knowing. It's part of the process. Learn as you go, but don't let it stop you from writing your story.

This whole idea of being good enough or obsessing over book sales wrapping around us so tightly that it's an indication of whether or not we're good enough, or consistent records or likes or followers or shares or reviews or...

Stop.

That will drive you absolutely bananas. But it will do more than that. It will stifle your creativity, your energy, and flow towards the positive light that is meant to surround this work.

Your work should reflect Jesus. Period. Your passion is to produce a work that would not only be pleasing to Him, but to also glorify Him.

He thinks you're enough. I had a teacher friend once who had a severe fear of not being able to write well so she decided to put off her dreams of becoming an author. When I told her the following truth, it hit her in a profound way, "God doesn't hold a red pen." She started blogging and was no longer worried about all of the messiness because she knew there was a message in there. She's touching lives today, through the work of the Holy Spirit, not because she writes in this fancy-smancy way, but because she gets right to the Word and to the truth of it, and speaks it like it is.

She has readers who follow her. She is gaining traction, but she would have never started if she would have lived with that spirit of fear.

*"For the Spirit God gave us does not make us timid, but gives us **power**, **love** and **self-discipline**." 2 Timothy 1:7*

———— ◦◯◦ ————

JOURNAL REFLECTION:

Take time to reflect over the Bible verse above and the gifts of the Holy Spirit and how they contribute to our author life.

Power:

Love:

Self-Discipline:

In what ways do we interfere with the power of the Holy Spirit to help us with our blank page?

I would love if you would pray over these following statements. You can speak them out loud. Right where you are. How about if you repeat after me.

I am enough.

I am good enough.

My story needs to be told.

Even if it's for only one person.

I will tell my story.

I will turn my blank page over to the Lord.

Amen.

Please repeat these facts as much as you can. If you start to get discouraged, remember, come back right here and stay awhile in 2 Timothy 1:7, journal again, pray, and ask the Lord to remove any stumbling blocks in your way, especially if that means your own doubt.

I would love to share with you a story I wrote about how I also struggled with the low self-concept of was my writing good enough. This was before I published and AFTER I published. Don't think this was easy for me, in fact, it was one of the hardest lessons I had to learn. I had to learn to let go and trust God. I hope you find comfort in this story. The message is that God knows the details of our lives right down to the very thread. He knows your desires of your author heart, too.

I WAS INVITED TO SPEAK at a women's meeting at my home church. I was beyond ecstatic that I'd have a chance to go back to visit with the women who prayed with me, loved me, sang with me and helped me find my singing voice, and supported me throughout my single parenting, to my new marriage and move. These women are part of my story. One woman in particular even inspired the theme of this devotional and many characters that I have in my books. If you ever read any and see the name Mrs. Rachel, then you'll know she was my church elder who I dearly love.

Mrs. Rachel is a lovely soul. She was the one that taught me about "God things." She battled brain cancer with a smile and a praise and worship song on her lips. She never gave up, and she taught me not to, either. Mrs. Rachel also looked to me with kind eyes at every meeting. The kind of look that lets you know you're good enough.

I wrote a middle grades romance, *My Boyfriend's Back: Angels in Love*, over the summer, right before going to the church meeting. I need to tell you about how Mrs. Rachel reappeared from my Holy Spirit to the page, back again with comedic flair, gracing the pages of my novel. She stopped with her truck in the parking lot of the church, hollering out to my young couple, making singing plans at her home to practice for a church song. Mrs. Rachel pulled out her butter tin filled with crocheted tea cozies in patterns specifically matching memories down to colors and designs. She encouraged and prayed for the main character every chance she could. It made a difference. It gave my character hope. It's the kind of hope that even can be felt from a fictional character and maybe plant a seed in a reader.

The morning of the meeting arrived. We drove for two hours for the breakfast event. I have to admit I wasn't nervous at all as I held my notes and Bible in my lap. All the way there I felt this expectation. A voice would say, "But you aren't good enough..." and I would push it aside. I planned to talk to them about how they will always be a part of my story and my author journey. They loved me enough to ask me to talk about how the Lord was using me with my books. I was ready. I was letting go and trusting God.

Because I trusted God, the voice had no room to take up space. God filled every space.

When we pulled up in the parking lot and stepped out of the car, here comes a truck. Yep, you can guess it. It's Mrs. Rachel, rolling down her window, exactly like the scene in my book. I wanted to cry that very second, and it took everything in me to hold it in. I told her, "You just don't know how this right here matters." It was as if God was whispering in the parking lot, "I told you so. I gave you that book. You are good enough. Your work matters. It matters to me."

I shared how much I loved the ladies of First Baptist and how their love and support have shaped who I am today. The elders are precious and every one of them have fingerprints on my heart. After I spoke, they passed me a gift bag. I was touched. I didn't expect a thing. Here I was, thanking them for all they've done for me, and they get me gifts.

I pull out two crocheted potholders. I look up and ask, "Who did this?"

You already know the answer.

Mrs. Rachel.

She crocheted them for me the night before because she felt led to do so. She had many colors to choose from, and the three colors she chose, she knew they were meant just for me. It was the color of my dress, coat, and my husband's shirt, all woven together. A memory of my first book talk. The first book talk I ever had, and I was holding proof in my hand that God knew and was proud of me for following His prompting, right down to the thread, for pushing the doubt away and going after my dreams and calling to serve Him with the words I could give.

God knows it all. God is there. He knows our every step. He knows our weakness, and He is our strength. When the voice tries to come back to me that says, "You aren't good enough," I am reminded of Mrs. Rachel and her "God thing" moments. Like the one we shared together, at the beginning and ending of my first book talk.

When I shared with her the role she played in the novel, crocheting colors based on memories, we stared at each other in awe.

I knew she would say it. It was coming. My Spirit was ready to receive it.

She glowed with a lovely smile, her face filled with the light of the Lord, and said, "It's a God thing."

Yes, Mrs. Rachel, it is.

CHALLENGE:

Grab a pack of sticky notes the next time you are out shopping. Leave yourself messages. Use them as bookmarks. Stick them on a mirror or your dashboard of your car. If you don't want to go the sticky note route, pull out your cellphone. Leave yourself reminders to randomly go off throughout the day, a particular hour, or set them on repeat.

Write words that will build you up. Words that will tell Satan, "Not today. Get behind me. I've got work to do for the Lord (Matthew 4:10)." Write words that say - I am enough (Philippians 4:13) I am a child of God (1 John 3:1). I am loved (John 3:16) I am beautifully and wonderfully made (Psalm 139:14). I am special in the eyes of God and He makes plans for me (Jeremiah 29:11). I am His chosen people, a royal priesthood (1 Peter 2:9). I am God's handiwork (Ephesians 2:10). I am thankful for my blessings (Philippians 4:6). Happy writing!

I challenge you (and myself) to continue working on this as the days go by. In the author world, we say we are currently working on our WIP or finishing or editing our WIP. We are all a Work in Progress. Let's not forget that. I haven't mastered this challenge yet, but I'm getting better. We need to know who we are in Christ, be encouraged, stay strong, and do not fear. The Lord is with us wherever we go (Joshua 1:9).

JOURNAL REFLECTION:

What if God has shown you "God things" in your every day, but if you might have a negative voice in your head, you might have missed the call? In your quiet time of prayer and reflection, pray upon verses that the Holy Spirit directs you to study. How can meditating on God's Word help build you up in times of doubt, worry, or fear? How can repeating His scripture help you to stand against the wiles of the devil? As you journal, copy Scripture along with your reflection. After writing Scripture and praying over God's Word, how do you feel? How can you apply this to your life throughout the day?

"Therefore go and
make disciples of all
nations,
baptizing them in the
name of the Father
and of the Son and of
the Holy Spirit,
and teaching them to
obey everything I
have commanded you.
And surely I am with
you always, to the
very end of the age."
Matthew 28:19-20

Obey the Call

Guiding Bible Verse: *"Therefore go and make disciples of all nations, baptizing them in the name of the Father and of the Son and of the Holy Spirit, and teaching them to obey everything I have commanded you. And surely I am with you always, to the very end of the age." Matthew 28:19-20*

This book is a challenge devotional that prepares the way for you to take the leap of faith required to honor your blank page. There are no gimmicks or tricks. I'm encouraging you to find who you are, your writing style, your voice, and the only way you can do that is to begin writing.

You can't edit something that is blank. You can't grow in your writing if you don't start. We all need practice. Writing takes time. You don't need a degree. You don't need fancy equipment. All you need is the time you can carve out to obey the call.

Give yourself the gift of time.

Challenge:

Create a writing routine. Give yourself grace through this process because life can happen and time may need to be rearranged, but challenge yourself to write every chance you get, preferably a little every day.

How do you know you're getting better at this writing stuff? We can be a little close to our own work and become biased. We also can fall in love with our story and our characters and sometimes can be blinded by the little sink holes we're creating.

How can we improve?

We continue to read in our genre. Reading well-written books with strong appeal and a wide audience is a great joy, but also a teaching tool.

Beta readers can also help inform you of your writing plot holes. My mom was the best beta reader around. She championed me fully and was all in with complete discussions, but she also wasn't afraid to speak her straight fact truth to me. I needed that. She'd tell me when a character wasn't believable. She'd question decisions and motivations of character and encourage me to rethink areas where the holes were too great to close up on their own. She'd find the missing gaps, and talk me through them. Find a trusted beta reader or a top-notch editor that can help you do the same thing.

I love to have beta readers come along for the ride with me. I don't give them the completed manuscript but give them chapter by chapter view so in case I goof, I can catch it early and I don't have to clean up so much mess later. That's just the way I do things, but that isn't the only way.

I set up a secret Facebook group to allow people I love in my circle a chance to be on my launch team. I've created beta reader teams of teachers, friends, and church members. I've included strangers in beta readings before, but felt as if it were better served for those who knew me, the genre in which I write, and the southern way my books always tend to navigate towards.

Editing comes last. I work that stuff tirelessly. I've had a couple of wonderful opened doors for editors, but mostly I edit with beta readers, teachers, and final copy edits are done by me, *ProWritingAid*, and my other friend *Grammarly*.

I've learned editing tips from other editors and authors online who are willing to share their expertise. Ellen Brock is my favorite YouTuber in the author world. She's also an editor. Bottom line: work your page. Write that thing. Then, go to beta readers and editors and get your rounds of edits started.

Trust this is a process. Trust this is a work in progress. We are all WIPs!

Each and every one of us.

And now you're ready to obey the call. Welcome to the author community. I'm so glad you're here.

JOURNAL REFLECTION:

How can you obey the call? What steps do you need to take to ensure that you're following God's lead and spreading your message God has laid upon your heart to deliver.

Thanks for Reading

I would love it if you could add a review online. Reviews can help spread the word about my work!

Thank you for all of your prayers and support.

I'd love to see your photos with my devotional! Please share social media reviews, and challenge others to pick up this devotional. Don't forget to tag me on social media so that I can join in on spreading the love around!

Join Jen Lowry's Patreon community at www.patreon.com/join/JenLowry[1] to be a part of a Christian writing community and have Jen as your personal writing coach.

---

1. http://www.patreon.com/join/JenLowry

About the Author

DR. JENNIFER IKNER Lowry is a proud native of Robeson County, North Carolina. She is the author of a YA contemporary fiction novel, Sweet Potato Jones (2020 with Swoon Romance) and thirteen titles ranging from children's picture books, middle grades, young adult to an adult holiday romance. You'll find her enjoying every second of life spent with her family (preferably in pajamas). If you ask her what she's reading it's probably more than one book. She's the CEO of Monarch Educational Services, L.L.C for authors, a homeschool momma to her two sweet boys, and full time Literacy Coach with Wake County Schools.

Website: www.jenlowrywrites.com

Twitter, Facebook, and IG @jenlowrywrites

Author's Note

If you, a friend, or a loved one needs help, please don't keep it inside.

There are family, guidance counselors, teachers, community and nationwide organizations that can offer help.

National Alliance on Mental Illness (NAMI):

https://www.nami.org/

1-800-950-6264

TEXT NAMI to 741741

National Suicide Prevention Hotline:

https://suicidepreventionlifeline.org/

1-800-273-8255

TEXT HOME to 741741

Atrium Health Call Center

1-704-444-2400

Mental Health Resources

http://www.mhresources.org

American Psychology Association

http://www.psychiatry.org/mental-health/

Don't miss out!

Visit the website below and you can sign up to receive emails whenever Jen Lowry publishes a new book. There's no charge and no obligation.

https://books2read.com/r/B-A-PFHI-LRQCB

BOOKS 2 READ

Connecting independent readers to independent writers.